History & Me

Dover Publications, Inc.
Mineola, New York

Bibliographical Note
History & Me, first published by Dover Publications, Inc., in 2015, contains
pages from the following online workbooks published by Education.com:
She's So Cool, American Heroes, Presidential Potpourri, Tracing Your Roots.

International Standard Book Number
ISBN-13: 978-0-486-80263-3
ISBN-10: 0-486-80263-9

Manufactured in the United States by Courier Corporation
80263901   2015
www.doverpublications.com

CONTENTS

CONTENTS

SHE'S SO COOL

What is a Biography?

In this section, you will both read and write biographies of famous women in history.

A biography is the true story of someone's life written by someone else. Most biographies include the following information:

- Where and when the person was born
- Family information
- Major life events such as education, marriage, children
- Life accomplishments
- Major accomplishments and their impact on society

When writing a biography it is important to include these facts along with other interesting details about a person's life.

Pretend someone is going to write a biography about you. Answer the following questions in complete sentences.

1. Where and when were you born?

_____

2. Who are the members of your immediate family?

_____

3. What is the most exciting thing you have ever done?

_____

_____

4. Describe a time that you were proud of something you accomplished.

_____

_____

_____

Reading for Comprehension:
Julia Morgan

Julia Morgan was an architect who designed buildings in California. She was the first woman to graduate from a famous architecture school in Paris, and the first woman to become an official architect in California.

After high school, where she had liked to study math, she went to Paris to enroll in a school that had a very good architecture program. However, she was turned away because she was a woman. After two years, she was finally let in and went on to become the school's first female architecture graduate.

Julia's first big project was to rebuild the Fairmont Hotel in San Francisco after it was damaged in the 1906 earthquake. Over the years, she designed more than 700 buildings, many of which are now considered historical treasures. Many of the buildings she designed were for businesses that helped women, like many YWCA buildings and a women's college in Oakland. She is perhaps most famous for designing Hearst Castle, a beautiful castle on the coast of California.

Answer these questions based on the passage.

1.   Where did Julia Morgan build her buildings?

_____

2.   What did she like to study in school?

_____

3.   Why did the school in Paris turn her down?

_____

4.   Why did the Fairmont Hotel in San Francisco need to be rebuilt?

_____

5.   What is Julia's most famous building?

_____

Finding the Main Idea:
Madam C.J. Walker

When reading a biography it is important to find the main ideas within the text. The main ideas will help you write a clear report.

Read the following passage about Madam C.J. Walker.

Madam C.J. Walker was the first woman to earn over one million dollars in America. Madam C.J. Walker was born Sarah Breedlove in Louisiana on December 23, 1867, just a few years after President Lincoln freed the slaves. Her parents had been slaves, and she was the first child in her family to be born a free woman.

When she was growing up, her family did not have a lot of money. She had a skin disease on her head that caused her to lose her hair, and suffered many years of hair loss. Determined to find a way to grow her hair back, she invented hair care products for African-American women. She used her husband's name – Charles J. Walker – and went around the country selling her products and showing people how to use them, and soon she made enough money to start a factory and a beauty school.

Madam C.J. Walker used a lot of the money she made to help African-Americans in her community, donating to organizations and community centers for African-Americans. Her beauty products are still sold today.

What is the main idea of the passage above?

_____

_____

_____

_____

Identifying Facts:
Hatshepsut

In non-fiction, all the information in the writing must be true. A piece of true information is called a *fact*.

Read the passage about Hatshepsut and find three facts.

Hatshepsut was a queen in ancient Egypt. She ruled Egypt for over 20 years, and the country thrived under her leadership.

Egypt's leaders were called pharaohs (*fare-ohs*). Hatshepsut was born around 1508 B.C to a pharaoh named Thutmose I. Only sons were allowed to become pharaohs. When Thutmose I died, power was passed to her half-brother, Thutmose II. 15 years later, Thutmose II died. Normally, this would have meant Hatshepsut's stepson, Thutmose III, would have become pharaoh, but he was only a baby. She took over as pharaoh while her stepson was a child. In the years that followed, she became a powerful leader.

While she was pharaoh, she decided to look the part. She wore traditional king's clothing, even a fake beard! Under her power, Egypt grew and grew. The arts flourished, new buildings were built, and voyages to other lands were carried out. New trade routes were started and the country made lots of money. She was a peaceful leader.

1. _____

2. _____

3. _____

Identifying Details:
Julia Child

Read this passage about Julia Child. When you're finished, write down 4 details about her life that made the story more interesting.

There was much more to Julia Child than met the eye! Julia Child was a famous chef who helped America discover glamorous French cooking. Before she was a famous chef, she worked for the government. In 1941, she volunteered to join the OSS. She played an important part in top-secret government missions, and traveled all over the world as a spy for the U.S. government. Two years later, her husband was sent to France on business. She went with him to France, where she fell in love with French cooking. She studied at France's most famous cooking school, and worked with talented chefs.

At the time, most Americans considered French food to be very expensive and not easy to cook at home. Together with her friends, she wrote a cookbook about French food, called *Mastering the Art of French Cooking*. Publishers didn't think anyone would want to read it – it was over 700 pages long! – but the book became a huge success in the United States.

After the success of the book, she went on a local television show in Boston to demonstrate how to cook an omelet. Viewers were so impressed that she decided to start her own cooking show. It was called *The French Chef*, and it showed her cooking recipes step-by-step so viewers could follow along. For the rest of her life, she hosted cooking shows and wrote many books, and helped people see cooking as not a chore, but as an art form.

1. _____

2. _____

3. _____

4. _____

Recording Facts:
Shakuntala Devi

When taking notes, it is important to record information in your own words. Copying what someone else has written is against the law.

Read this biography of Shakuntala Devi.

Shakuntala Devi was known as "The Human Computer." When she was very young, her father tried to teach her card tricks. However, she would always beat him because she could remember all the numbers in the cards she was shown! Within the next year, she was showing off her skills at local schools, and was a famous math whiz by her teens. When she figured out a problem, she was often faster than a computer. In 1977, she found out the 23rd root of a 201-digit number (in other words, a really tough math problem!) in less than a minute. She made history again in 1980, when she multiplied two 13-digit numbers in just 28 seconds. She was put in the 1982 *Guinness Book of World Records* for her talent.

Rewrite the sentences from this paragraph in your own words. The first two sentences have been done for you.

1.   *Shakuntala Devi's nickname was "The Human Computer."*

2.   *When she was young, her father tried to teach her card tricks.*

3.

4.

5.

6.

7.

8.

Text Features:
Female FSA Photographers

During the Great Depression, many workers in America lost their jobs. The government started a program called the Farm Security Administration, or the FSA, to help those that needed it. As part of the program, they sent out a team of photographers to take pictures of struggling families, and later, of daily life during World War II. Many of the photographers were women.

The most famous woman on the team was Dorothea Lange. Her photograph, "Migrant Mother," is the most famous photo taken during that time. Marion Post Wolcott was another FSA photographer. Before she started with them, she had been working as a newspaper photographer. She was frustrated with her work, because she was always being asked to photograph "ladies' stories" like fashion shows. However, her photographer friends believed in her, and convinced the person hiring photographers for the FSA to hire her. A similar thing happened to Louise Rosskam: when she and her husband, also a photographer, both applied to a magazine, they hired him but refused to hire her. They both later found jobs with the FSA. Ann Rosener liked to take photos of women working in factories and other "men's" jobs to support their families.

The women that worked for the FSA showed the world that photography could do more than just make people look pretty – it could be used to reveal problems in the world and help change peoples' minds about important issues.

Write 3 things that you can tell about the Great Depression by looking at the picture.

1. _____

2. _____

3. _____

Text Features:
Deborah Sampson

In non-fiction writing, you will often find different text features. Subheadings are used to divide long passages into smaller pieces. Subheadings are usually bold. Footnotes give extra information about something within a passage. A small number or mark will show that there is a footnote at the bottom of the page.

Read the biography of Deborah Sampson and highlight or circle the subheadings and footnotes.

Early Life

Deborah Sampson was born on December 17th, 1760 in Plympton, Massachusetts. She was one of seven children, and was part of a family that had sailed to Plymouth in the Mayflower. At the age of ten, she was sent away to work on a farm. On the farm, she did a lot of hard work all day.

Deborah in Disguise

In Deborah Sampson's time, only men were allowed to be soldiers. When the American Colonies went to war with Britain, Deborah wanted to help her country. She disguised herself as a man and joined the army. She fought alongside men for months and no one knew her secret, until she was hurt and had to see a doctor. The doctor found out her true identity, but he kept her secret. Shortly after, she received an honorable discharge[1] and was sent home.

The Fight's Not Over

After being sent home, she did not receive her pay. Male soldiers were paid a pension[2], but she was not paid at all. She wrote a complaint that was heard by the Senate. Founding fathers like Paul Revere and John Hancock supported her, and helped convince their colleagues that she deserved to be paid the same amount as her fellow soldiers. She won, and was given the money she was owed.

A Lasting Legacy

Deborah's actions changed peoples' minds about what women can do both on and off the battlefield. Now, both men and women serve side-by-side in the armed forces.

1: When a good soldier is allowed to leave service, it is called an honorable discharge.
2: A payment that is given every month.

Reading a Timeline:
Sojourner Truth

Read the timeline about Sojourner Truth.

c. 1797: Sojourner Truth is born a slave with the name Isabella Baumfree.

1815: Marries another slave named Thomas.

1815-1826: Has five children: Diana, James, Peter, Elizabeth, and Sophia.

1826: She and her daughter Sophia escape to freedom.

1826: She finds out that her son, Peter, was illegally sold to another owner. She stood up to the owner in court and won her son back, becoming one of the first African-American women to win a case against a Caucasian man.

1829: Moves to New York City and takes a job as a housekeeper to earn money for her family.

1843: Changes her name to Sojourner Truth.

1850: Her biography, *The Narrative of Sojourner Truth: A Northern Slave,* is published.

1850: Gives her first speech about slavery and human rights.

1851: Delivers her most famous speech, "Ain't I a Woman?" at the Ohio Women's Rights Convention

1851-1853: Tours Ohio giving talks about human and women's rights.

1860s: Sojourner helps recruit African-American men to fight for the Union during the Civil War.

Answer the following questions using the timeline.

1.   What year did Sojourner Truth escape? _____

2.   What happened to Sojourner Truth in 1850? _____

3.   Why do you think she wanted rights for women as well as an end to slavery?

_____

4.   What do you think is the most important event in her life? Circle it on the timeline.

Create a Timeline

Interview a parent or grandparent and create a timeline of their life using this sheet. Use the Sojourner Truth timeline as an example.

Year: _____ **Event:** _____

_____

_____

Year: _____ **Event:** _____

_____

_____

Year: _____ **Event:** _____

_____

_____

Year: _____ **Event:** _____

_____

_____

Year: _____ **Event:** _____

_____

_____

Year: _____ **Event:** _____

_____

_____

Comparing Two People:
Bessie Coleman
and
Mae Jemison

Read these biographies of Bessie Coleman and Mae Jemison, then turn the page.

Bessie Coleman

Before there was Amelia Earhart, there was Bessie Coleman. Bessie Coleman was the first African-American woman to get a pilot's license and a pioneering female aviator who became famous for her daring air show stunts in the 1920s.

Bessie Coleman was born on January 26, 1892 in Atlanta, Texas. Bessie grew up in Texas, then moved to Chicago with her family at age 23. She worked as a manicurist in a barbershop. While working in the shop, she overheard stories told by men who had flown planes in World War I. She wanted to try flying for herself. She applied to flight schools, but no one would teach her because she was both a woman and African-American. She decided to go to Paris to find a school that would teach her.

After getting her license, Bessie wanted to start a flying school just for African-Americans. To raise money to start the school, she began working as a stunt pilot. People would come out to watch her fly planes in all kinds of crazy directions: Figure eights, loop-de-loops, and steep drops. Bessie soon became known as "Queen Bess," and within five years she was a popular air show performer.

Mae Jemison

Mae Jemison was the first African-American woman to go to space. Mae was born on October 17, 1956, the youngest of three children. Growing up, Mae loved science. She studied medicine in college and started her career as a doctor, going around the world to care for those in need.

In 1983, Mae applied to NASA. Mae was inspired by Sally Ride's first flight a few years before, and also by the character of Uhura from *Star Trek* (the character was an African-American officer on a spaceship). Mae's first application was denied, but she didn't give up! She applied a second time and in 1987, she was hired. Five years later, she flew on the STS-47 mission to study life in space. She even brought a picture of Bessie Coleman with her to inspire her on the flight.

Mae retired from NASA in 1993. She went on to start scientific research companies, and she even got to be on an episode of her favorite TV show, *Star Trek: The Next Generation*. She accomplished a first there too – the first real astronaut to ever be on the show.

Comparing Two Famous People

One way to compare two people is by using a Venn diagram. A Venn diagram uses circles to represent sets of information. These circles overlap. The overlapping area is used to record things that are the same about the two sets, while the outside areas are used to record things that are different.

Reread the text about Bessie Coleman and Mae Jemison and complete the Venn diagram below.

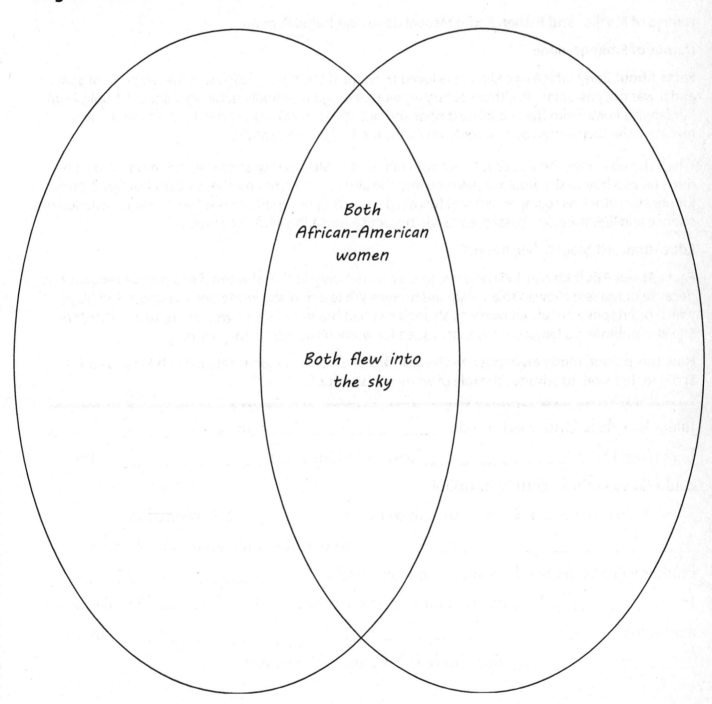

Both
African-American
women

Both flew into
the sky

Using Notes to Write:
Juana Ines de la Cruz

Below is an example of a complete biography outline. Use the information in the outline to complete the paragraph about Juana Ines de la Cruz.

Famous Person's Name: Juana Ines de la Cruz

Date and Place of Birth: November 12, 1651, San Miguel Nepantla, Mexico

Names of Mother and Father: Pedro Manuel de Asbaje, Isabel Ramirez

Names of Siblings: none

Facts About Early Life: As a child, Juana loved to learn. At the time, Mexico was the property of Spain, and it was not customary in either country for women to go to school. Juana would sneak books from her family's library into the chapel next door and hide there, reading in secret. By the time she was a teenager, she had written poetry, could do math, and had learned Latin.

When she was older, she was sent to live with her aunt in Mexico City. She asked her mother to let her dress up as a boy so she would be allowed into the city's schools. Her mother said no, but hired a tutor for her. Her tutor was so impressed that he called a meeting of experts to test her on her knowledge of science and literature. She passed, and soon became a sensation in Mexico City.

Education: Self-taught, then tutored

Facts About Adult Life: In 1667, she became a nun not only so that she could explore her religion, but because nuns were allowed to educate themselves. While a nun, she wrote books, poems, and plays, which often spoke out about women's struggles or had brave and smart women as main characters. She also published a famous essay that argued for women's access to education.

How this person made an impact on the world: She is now a national hero in both Mexico and Spain for her work to advance the role of women in society.

Juana Ines de la Cruz was born on _____ in _____.
Juana loved to _____ and had to hide in a _____ so she could do so without getting in trouble.

When she was older, she was sent to live in _____ . She wanted to
_____ so that she could go to school, but her
mother wouldn't let her. Instead, her mother hired a _____.
In _____, she became a nun so that she would be allowed to study. While she was
a nun, she wrote _____, _____, and
_____ that showed smart and brave women.

Transition Words:
Ada Lovelace

Transition words help a story flow smoothly. Some transition words are: *after, later, last, until, since, then, before, when, once, about, during, next* and *now*.

Read the short biography of Ada Lovelace. Highlight all of the transition words that are used in the passage.

Ada Lovelace was born in 1815 in London to Anne Isabella Byron and the famous poet, Lord Byron. When she was a child, her mother encouraged her to study math, which was unusual for a woman at the time. In 1833, she met mathematician Charles Babbage at a party. Charles had been making a machine that could calculate math problems. Once he found out she was interested in math, they became good friends. He showed the machine to her and she was fascinated by it. Charles then took Ada under his wing and taught her about his research during the next several years.

About ten years later, Charles had an idea for a new mathematical machine. A fellow scientist had written an article about it, but it was written in French. Charles asked Ada to translate the article for him. Not only did she translate the article, she added her own notes and ideas. Many of her ideas are still used in computers today. Her work went unnoticed until many years later, when scientists realized how revolutionary her ideas were. Now, she is considered by many to be the world's first computer programmer.

Biography Note Taking Sheet

Find a biography of a woman you admire or would like to know more about. Take notes on the sheet below.

Famous Person's Name: _____

Date and Place of Birth: _____ _____

Names of Mother and Father: _____ _____

Names of Siblings: _____

Interesting Facts About Early Life:

_____

_____

_____

Schooling:

_____

_____

Interesting Facts About Adult Life:

_____

_____

_____

How This Person Made an Impact on the World:

_____

_____

_____

_____

Writing a Biography

Using what you have learned in this book, write a short biography of the woman you took notes on earlier. Make sure to include all the details mentioned on the first page and a bibliography at the end. Draw or glue a picture of your subject in the box at the top.

_____
Name

Cite Your Sources

An important part of research is giving credit to the sources that you use. This is called *citing your sources*. A final list of sources used in a research paper is called a *bibliography*.

When sources are organized into a bibliography, they must be in alphabetical order. Refer to the table below to properly cite your sources.

Type of Reference	Information Needed for Bibliography
Book	Author's Last Name, Author's First Name. Title of Book. City of Publication: Publisher, Date of Publication.
Book with Two Authors	Author's Last Name, Author's First Name and Author Last Name, Author First Name. Title of Book. City of Publication: Publisher, Date of Publication.
Magazine	Author's Last name, Author's First Name. "Title of Article". Magazine Title. Date: Page Number.
Website	Author's Last Name, Author's First Name. "Title of Article". The Title of the Website. Date You Visited. <Website URL>
Encyclopedia Article	"Title of Article." Name of the Encyclopedia. Volume Number. City Where the Book Was Published: Name of the Publisher, Year Book was Published.

Presentation Ideas

After completing your biography report, you may want to present what you have learned. Here are some examples of how to make your presentation fun and interesting.

- **Interview Your Subject:** Create a paper bag puppet of the person you researched and wrote a report on. Then, create questions to ask the puppet based on what you learned. During the presentation you will talk to the puppet and the puppet will answer.

- **Become a Historic Figure:** Do a little research on what your historical figure looked like and what they may have worn. On the day of the presentation, dress as the person and present your report as if you are that figure.

- **Write Creatively:** Compose a song or write a poem to sing or read to your audience about your subject.

- **Tell the Story through Props:** Create several "artifacts" and gather props that help tell the story of the person you have researched.

- **Make a Diorama:** Create a few 3D scenes from the person's life so that others can get a view of what their life was like.

- **Try Your Hand:** Put yourself in your subject's shoes by doing the thing they were famous for. Find a Julia Child recipe and cook it, design a house like Julia Morgan, or concoct a new shampoo like Madam C.J. Walker!

Great job!

is an Education.com writing superstar

AMERICAN
HEROES

Abraham Lincoln

Abraham Lincoln was the 16th President of the United States. He became President in 1861. He was President during the Civil War and helped keep the Union from splitting into two countries. In 1863, he signed the Emancipation Proclamation, the document that set all American slaves free.

Word scramble!

Unscramble the letters to form the word that completes the sentence.

1. Lincoln was born in the state of _____ .   UNEKTCYK

2. Lincoln once worked as a _____ .   EALYRW

3. Lincoln's wife's name was _____ .   AMYR

John Adams..

John Adams

John Adams was the second President of the United States. He was a delegate to the Continental Congress, which governed the colonies before they became the United States of America. Adams helped the United States become independent from Britain.

Word scramble!

Unscramble the letters to form the word that completes the sentence.

1. Adams was also the first _____ President.

   IVEC

2. Adams' son, John _____ Adams, was the 6th President of the United States.

   YUQICN

3. Adams was the only one of the first five Presidents who did not own _____ .

   ELSAVS

Alexander Hamilton

Alexander Hamilton, one of America's Founding Fathers, had a key role in writing the Constitution of the United States. His ideas about government shaped the Constitution, as well as the government we have today. All of the States had to accept the Constitution before it became official, and Hamilton was mostly responsible for convincing his home state of New York to sign on. He was also the nation's first Secretary of the Treasury.

Word scramble!

Unscramble the letters to form the word that completes the sentence.

1. Hamilton fought on the side of the American colonies in the _____ War. IONVOLUTARYRE

2. He fought under General George _____ , who was so impressed that he gave Hamilton a job as his aide.   HINWAGTSON

3. Hamilton wanted to create a strong _____ , or national, government for the United States.   ALEFRDE

Eleanor Roosevelt

Eleanor Roosevelt was born in 1884. She was a writer and a humanitarian, a person who works to help the poor and disadvantaged. She spoke out for human rights, equality for all, and children's causes. To help women gain equal rights in a time when they had few, President John F. Kennedy made her the leader of a special group called the Presidential Commission on the Status of Women.

Word scramble!

Unscramble the letters to form the word that completes the sentence.

1. Eleanor was also the wife of President _____ D. Roosevelt.

   LIRANFNK

2. Her humanitarian work changed the way America thought about what a _____ Lady could be.

   STIRF

3. Roosevelt spoke for the U.S. as a member of the _____ Nations, a group of countries from around the world who work for peace and security for all nations.

   EDNIUT

Susan B. Anthony

Susan B. Anthony

Susan B. Anthony was born in Massachusetts in 1820. A civil rights leader, she is best known for helping women win the right to vote in the United States. In 1872, Anthony was one of the first women ever to vote in a Presidential election in the United States. Though she did not live to see it pass, the 19th Amendment gave women the right to vote on August 18, 1920.

She believed in equal rights for all people living in the United States, and she spoke out and worked against slavery.

Word scramble!

Unscramble the letters to form the word that completes the sentence.

1. The right of women to vote in elections is called women's _____ .   FUAGFRSE

2. Anthony helped pass the 13th Amendment, which _____ , or freed,
   all of the slaves.   ATEANEMPCID

3. In the last public speech of her life, Anthony inspired those working for women's
   rights by saying, "Failure is _____ ."   OSIMPBLESI

Lorraine Hansberry

Playwright
and author

Lorraine Hansberry was born in Chicago, Illinois in 1930. When she was still a small child, Hansberry's family moved to a restricted neighborhood for white residents, which was against the law at the time. Hansberry's father took the family's case all the way to the Supreme Court, and her mother stayed to guard the home, ready to defend her children if necessary. The family won their case, but the experience affected Hansberry deeply. Her best-known work, a dramatic play called A Raisin in the Sun, was inspired by these events. It was the first play written by an African-American to be produced on Broadway. At the age of 29, Hansberry became the youngest American playwright to receive the prestigious New York Drama Critics Circle Award for Best Play. Hansberry's promising career was cut short by her death from pancreatic cancer at the age of 34.

Word scramble!

Unscramble the letters to form the word that completes the sentence.

1. A Raisin in the Sun was also the first play on Broadway with an African-American
   _____ , Lloyd Richards.   TORREDIC

2. The 1961 film version of A Raisin in the Sun starred legendary African-American
   actor Sydney _____ .   OIIEPTR

3. A 2004 Broadway revival of A Raisin in the Sun, starring Sean "_____"
   Combs, received a Tony Award nomination for Best Revival of a Play.   YIDDD

Maya Angelou

Writer,
producer,
performer,
professor

Maya Angelou was born in St. Louis, Missouri in 1928. As a young woman, she joined Martin Luther King, Jr. and other leaders to establish Civil Rights organizations and work for equality for African-Americans. She was devastated when King was assassinated on April 4, 1968, which also happened to be her birthday. To begin dealing with her grief, she wrote the first of seven autobiographical volumes, <u>I Know Why the Caged Bird Sings</u>. The book won international acclaim, and she went on to become a successful writer, producer, actor and teacher. In 2010, President Barack Obama announced that Angelou would receive the Presidential Medal of Freedom, the highest civilian award in the United States.

Word scramble!

Unscramble the letters to form the word that completes the sentence.

1. Maya Angelou was born in St. Louis, _____ .   SMOIISUR

2. Her most famous work is I Know Why the _____ Bird Sings.   AGCDE

3. In 2010, she received the Presidential Medal of _____ .   RFMEDEO

Celia Cruz

Celia Cruz was born in Cuba, and became a citizen of the United States in 1959. She was a well-known singer of salsa songs, and introduced Cuban music to the people of the United States. She won seven Grammy Awards, the most important awards in American music. She received the National Medal of the Arts award in 1994.

Word scramble!

Unscramble the letters to form the word that completes the sentence.

1. Cruz recorded albums with some of the most famous musicians in _____ music.

   NLIAT

2. "Salsa" is not only the name for a kind of music, but also for a kind of _____ .

   ACEDN

3. Cuba is an island nation in a part of the ocean called the _____ Sea.

   EANACBRIB

Rosa Parks

In 1955, one woman's refusal to give up her seat on a bus helped end segretation on public buses. That woman was Rosa Parks, and when she disobeyed a bus driver who ordered her to give her seat to a white passenger, she was arrested and taken to jail. Though other African-Americans had bravely refused to give up their seats on buses in the past, it was the Montgomery Bus Boycott, led in part by Rosa Parks, that helped end segregation on public transportation.

Word scramble!

Unscramble the letters to form the word that completes the sentence.

1. Until the boycott, African-Americans in Alabama had to sit at the _____ of the bus.   AKBC

2. Rosa Parks became one of the most important leaders of the _____ Rights movement.   LIIVC

3. African-Americans were also banned from eating at some _____ , and from many other places.   TAREURANTSS

Frederick Douglass

Frederick Douglass

Frederick Douglass was a leader in the abolitionist movement, which fought to end slavery within the United States in the time leading up to the Civil War. Douglass was born a slave, but he escaped to the North, where slavery did not exist. He helped create an anti-slavery newspaper called The North Star.

Word scramble!

Unscramble the letters to form the word that completes the sentence.

1. Douglass sometimes gave President _____ advice.   LILNONC

2. He wanted to give African-Americans the right to _____ .   TVEO

3. Douglass was ambassador to the nation of _____ .   IAHIT

Booker T. Washington

Booker T. Washington was born into slavery on April 5, 1856. After the emancipation of the slaves, Washington was forced to get a job at age 9 to help support his poor family. In 1881, Washington became the Principal of Tuskegee Institute, a college for African-Americans in Tuskegee, Alabama. The school is still around today and is now called Tuskegee University. Washington wanted a good education for all African-Americans, and he worked his whole life to achieve this goal.

Word scramble!

Unscramble the letters to form the word that completes the sentence.

1. Booker T. Washington wrote a famous book about his life growing up, called "Up From _____".

   LAVSRYE

2. Though she herself could not read or write, Washington's _____ bought him textbooks so he could learn.

   ERMTHO

3. As a slave, Washington worked on a _____ , the type of farm on which most slaves were forced to work.

   NLANPIOTAT

Jesse Owens

Olympic Gold Medal-winning track and field athlete

James Cleveland Owens was born in Oakville, Alabama in 1913 He was nine years old when his family moved to Cleveland, Ohio, where he received the nickname Jesse. When his new teacher asked his name, he replied that it was "J.C.," as he was called at the time. Because of his Southern accent, the teacher misheard the name as "Jesse," and the nickname stuck.

As a boy, Owens took what odd jobs he could find, working while training on the track and field team in junior high school. Owens' coach allowed him to practice before school so he could keep his after-school job at a shoe repair shop. After high school, he went on to compete for Ohio State University's track team. He set three world records and tied a fourth. Still, he was forced to live off campus with other African-American athletes, and when the team traveled, he stayed in "black-only" hotels. Despite those circumstances, he persisted in his training and competition and went on to win four gold medals in the 1936 Olympic Games in Germany.

Word scramble!

Unscramble the letters to form the word that completes the sentence.

1. Jesse Owens was on the _____ _____ _____ team in high school.

   CTARK DAN EIFDL

2. Jesse was such a good athlete he set three world _____ .

   ERRODCS

3. Jesse won four gold _____ in the 1936 Olympics.

   ELMADS

W.E.B. Du Bois

Activist, journalist, sociologist

William Edward Burghardt Du Bois was born in Great Barrington, Massachusetts in 1868. Du Bois' father left the family before his second birthday, and his mother suffered a stroke when Du Bois was still a young child. He was forced to work to support himself and his mother, who could no longer work following her stroke. Despite this hardship, Du Bois remained focused on his studies, believing that his education could better their lives. He earned a degree from Fisk University, a historically African-American college in Nashville, Tennessee, then received a scholarship to Harvard. In 1895, he became the first African-American to earn a Ph.D. from Harvard University.

He taught at the university level for several years, then went to work at Atlanta University, now called Clark Atlanta University, in Atlanta, Georgia. He created the university's department of social work, which exists today as the Whitney M. Young, Jr. School of Social Work. He became founder and editor of the NAACP's journal, The Crisis, which published African-American writers, including some who wrote during the Harlem Renaissance. He argued against Booker T. Washington's belief that African-Americans should accept segregation and the idea that they could be "separate but equal."

Word scramble!

Unscramble the letters to form the word that completes the sentence.

1. Du Bois worked to disprove the theory that African-Americans were biologically inferior to white Americans, called _____ racism.   ICCIENSFTI

2. Du Bois was one of the founders of the NAACP, the National Association for the _____ of Colored People.   NTDVAEAEMNC

3. In 1950, Du Bois ran for U.S. _____ from New York as a member of the American Labor Party.   EOSRNAT

Martin Luther King, Jr.

Civil Rights leader

Martin Luther King, Jr. was born in Atlanta, Georgia in 1929. The son of a Baptist minister, he became one himself after studying at a theological seminary in Pennsylvania. There, he learned about the non-violent methods used by Mohandas Gandhi in protest of British colonization in India. King believed that African-Americans could gain their civil rights through peaceful demonstration and protest. He believed in methods such as the boycott, refusing to buy products or services from companies or people who discriminated against African-Americans.

In 1963, a civil rights march on Washington, D.C., called the March on Washington for Jobs and Freedom, helped make King internationally known. It was on the occasion of this march that King made his famous 'I Have A Dream' speech. He won the Nobel Peace Prize in 1964. That same year, the Civil Rights Act was passed, banning many types of discrimination against African-Americans.

Word scramble!

Unscramble the letters to form the word that completes the sentence.

1. Martin Luther King, Jr. was the son of a Baptist _____ .   MTIISERN

2. In school, he was inspired by Mohandas _____ .   GHNADI

3. He believed in non-violent methods like _____ .   OBYCTTO

George Washington Carver

Scientist, botanist and inventor

George Washington Carver was born into slavery some time between 1861 and 1864. No record exists to confirm the date of his birth. After the abolition of slavery, Carver's former masters, Moses and Susan Carver, raised George and his brother James as their own sons, teaching them reading and writing and encouraging George's intellectual pursuits. George took his new parents' last name.

A teacher at Simpson College in Iowa, where Carver was enrolled, noticed his talent for drawing flowers and encouraged him to study botany. Carver then went to study at Iowa State Agricultural College, where, to distinguish himself from another student named George Carver, he added Washington to his name. After a master's degree at Agricultural College, Booker T. Washington invited Carver to lead the agricultural department at the famed Tuskegee Institute. He remained there for 47 years, teaching former slaves farming techniques so they could support themselves.

Carver taught his students and agricultural professionals that crop rotation, the practice of planting different crops in the same fields year to year, could help soil retain its nutrients. He created many non-food products, everything from shaving cream to shoe polish to shampoo, from plants such as peanuts, sweet potatoes and pecans.

Word scramble!

Unscramble the letters to form the word that completes the sentence.

1. Though he is often falsely credited with having invented _____ _____ , Carver did create more than 300 products using peanuts.

   UTAPEN RUTBET

2. Carver's birthplace was declared a national _____ , the first ever dedicated to an African-American.

   NTMEONUM

3. Many leaders consulted with Carver over agricultural matters, from Presidents of the United States to the Crown Prince of the country of _____ .

   ESENWD

Lewis and Clark

On May 14, 1804, Meriwether Lewis, William Clark and a team of 31 others set out on an expedition from St. Louis, Missouri. Their goal was to explore the lands and rivers of the western United States. At that time, the United States had no maps of that land or its rivers. President Thomas Jefferson hoped to find a Northwest Passage, a route of rivers that ships could use to cross from east to west. The team finally reached the Pacific Ocean in November of 1805, completing their expedition.

Word scramble!

Unscramble the letters to form the word that completes the sentence.

1. Another goal of the expedition was to make friends and set up trade with _____ American tribes .   TNAEIV

2. _____ , a Native American woman who knew the territory, helped guide the expedition.   AWAGEASAC

3. Along the way, Lewis and Clark saw many kinds of plants and _____ they had never seen before.   ALSMANI

Benjamin Franklin

Benjamin Franklin was a man of many talents. A scientist, author printer and inventor, he wrote a famous book called <u>Poor Richard's Almanac</u>, which is still being published today. An almanac is a book of important facts, such as weather reports, recipes and advice, printed yearly. He was the inventor of many things we still use today, like the lightning rod, bifocal glasses, a heater called the Franklin stove, and even swim fins!

Word scramble!

Unscramble the letters to form the word that completes the sentence.

1. Using a metal key tied to a kite, Franklin proved that lightning conducts

   _ _ _ _ _ _ _ _ _ _ _ _ _ _ .   ITYLECECTRI

2. Franklin is responsible for the famous saying, "A penny saved is a penny

   _ _ _ _ _ _ _ _ _ _ _ _ _ _ _ ."   NEDEAR

3. Franklin believed all people should be free, and spoke out against the practice

   of _ _ _ _ _ _ _ _ _ _ _ _ _ .   YLASRVE

Thomas Edison

Thomas Edison was a scientist and inventor born in 1847. He is best known for his work with electric power. He invented a way to send power into homes and factories, and built a power station that created the electricity he sold. Edison helped design a type of light bulb similar to the one we use today, and he made many other discoveries in the field of electricity. He even invented a battery that could be used to power an electric car!

Word scramble!

Unscramble the letters to form the word that completes the sentence.

1. Edison created one of the first electric _____ , or power companies.   TIIESULIT

2. He had over 1,000 _____ , which give rights and credit for inventions to their creator.   PNTSATE

3. Edison also invented new ways of filming a _____ _____ , also known as a movie.   TIOMNO UPREICT

41

Great job!

_____

is an Education.com reading superstar

PRESIDENTIAL
POTPOURRI

George Washington

Finding the Facts

George Washington is known as the "Father of Our Country". Read about George Washington to see why he was given this nickname. After you read, complete the sentences.

George Washington was born in Virginia on February 22, 1732. At this time, America was ruled by England. When he was a young boy, George had to travel a very long distance to get to school. To get to his first school, George had to walk seven miles each way. George studied hard and became a surveyor. A surveyor is someone who measures land and makes maps. George Washington's home was a farm called Mount Vernon. As an adult, he married a woman named Martha Custis. Martha had two children, and George helped raise them. At this time, there were a lot of people living in America who did not want America to be part of England anymore. George Washington was chosen to be the Commander in Chief of the American army. He fought in the Revolutionary War so that America could be a separate country. After a long and difficult fight, America won the war and gained its independence from England. It became the United States of America, and George Washington was elected as the first president in 1789. At that time, the capital of the United States was New York. The capital later became Washington, D.C., named for George Washington.

1) When George Washington was born, America was ruled by _____ .

2) George Washington's first job was as a surveyor. A surveyor is someone who

_____ .

3) George Washington's home was called _____ .

4) Martha Custis was the _____ of George Washington.

5) George Washington was the Commander in Chief of

the_____ army.

46

George Washington's Life

Match the correct year and event with the space on the timeline. Draw a line from each event to its correct box on the timeline.

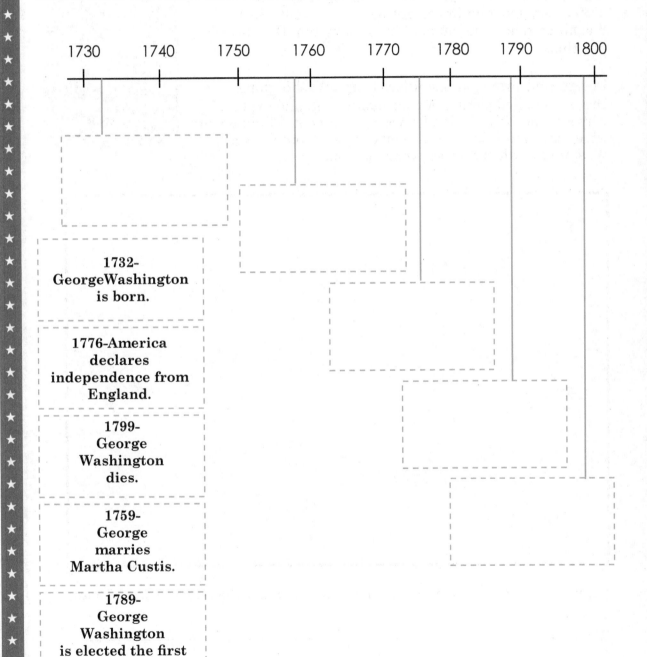

1730   1740   1750   1760   1770   1780   1790   1800

1732-GeorgeWashington is born.

1776-America declares independence from England.

1799-George Washington dies.

1759-George marries Martha Custis.

1789-George Washington is elected the first president of the U.S.

George Washington

Design a Monument

A monument is a sculpture or a building that helps people remember an important person or event. George Washington has a monument in Washington, D.C. It looks like this.

Design your own monument for George Washington. Draw a detailed picture of your monument, and explain why you chose the design for your monument. Think about what you want people to remember most about George Washington when they see your monument.

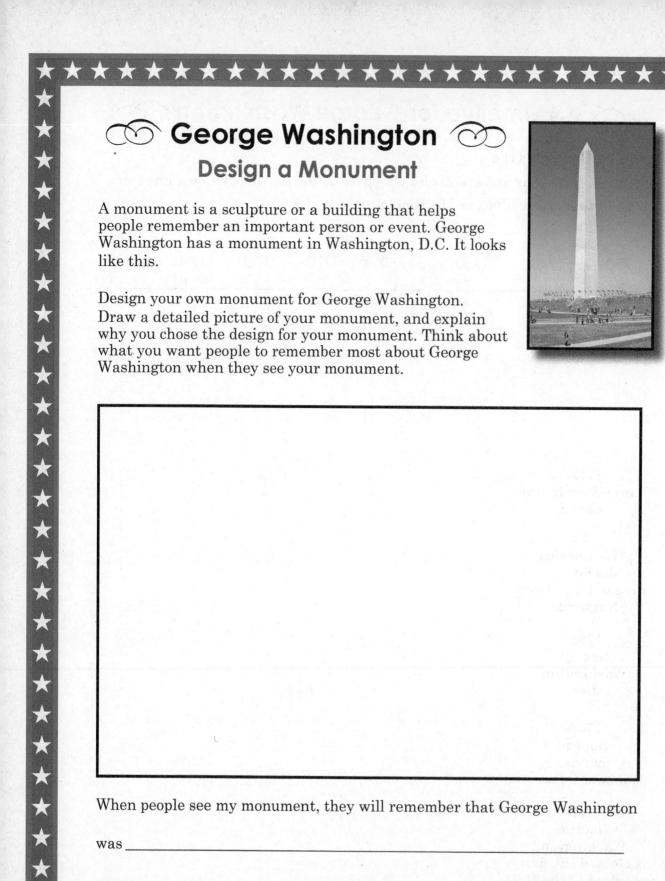

When people see my monument, they will remember that George Washington

was _____

_____ .

Painting a Portrait of President Washington

Use the color key to color this portrait of George Washington.

KEY
1-blue 2-white 3-black 4-peach 5-red 6-gray

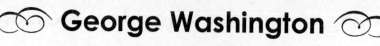 George Washington

You Tell the Story

You will be writing a biography on George Washington. First, organize your ideas. The topic sentence is done for you.

Topic Sentence: George Washington was called the "Father of our Country." List 3 main ideas that explain why Washington was the "Father of our Country."

_____

Main idea 1:_____

Main idea 2:_____

Main idea 3:_____

Concluding idea: Use new words to repeat the most important fact about George Washington. Why was he the "Father of Our Country"?

Example:

Topic Sentence: George Washington was called the "Father of Our Country."

Main idea 1: He was the Commander In Chief of the American Army.

Main idea 2: He won the Revolutionary War so we could be independent from England.

Main idea 3: He was the first president of the United States.

Concluding idea: George Washington was a very important man in the history of our country.

⚬⚬ George Washington ⚬⚬

You Tell the Story

Now it is time to put your ideas together.

George Washington was _____

Topic Sentence

_____ .

First, he _____

Main idea 1

_____ .

He also _____

Main idea 2

_____ .

Last, he _____

Main idea 3

_____ .

As you can see, _____

Concluding idea

_____

_____ .

∽ Abraham Lincoln ∽

Finding the Facts

Abraham Lincoln was our 16th president and often called "Honest Abe." Read about Abraham Lincoln to learn why he is one of our most well-known presidents. After you read, complete the sentences.

Abraham Lincoln was born in a log cabin the state of Kentucky on February 12, 1809. He and his sister worked on their family farm. When his family moved to Indiana, Abe helped build the family's new home. Abe didn't get to go to school very often, but he loved to read, and he would walk miles to borrow books. When he grew up, Abe had many different jobs. He was a shopkeeper and a mailman. Finally, Abe decided to study law, became a lawyer, and moved to Springfi eld, Illinois. There, he married Mary Todd. Abe and Mary had four children. In 1860, Abraham Lincoln was elected to be our 16th president. While he was president, the Civil War began. Our country was divided. The northern states were fi ghting against the southern states. During the war, Abraham Lincoln wrote the Emancipation Proclamation, which freed slaves. He also wrote a very famous speech called the Gettysburg Address. President Lincoln gave this speech to try to keep the United States together. The war lasted fi ve years, and President Lincoln was killed just fi ve days after the war ended. The United States had lost their president. and President Lincoln was killed just fi ve days after the war ended. The United States had lost their president.

1) Abraham Lincoln was born in a _____.

2) More than anything, Abraham Lincoln loved to _____ .

3) Abraham Lincoln studied law and became a _____ .

4) Abraham Lincoln was elected to be our _____ president in 1860.

5) Lincoln was president during the _____War.

A Timeline for Abraham Lincoln

Abraham Lincoln's Life

Match the correct year and event with the space on the timeline. Draw a line from each event to its correct box on the timeline.

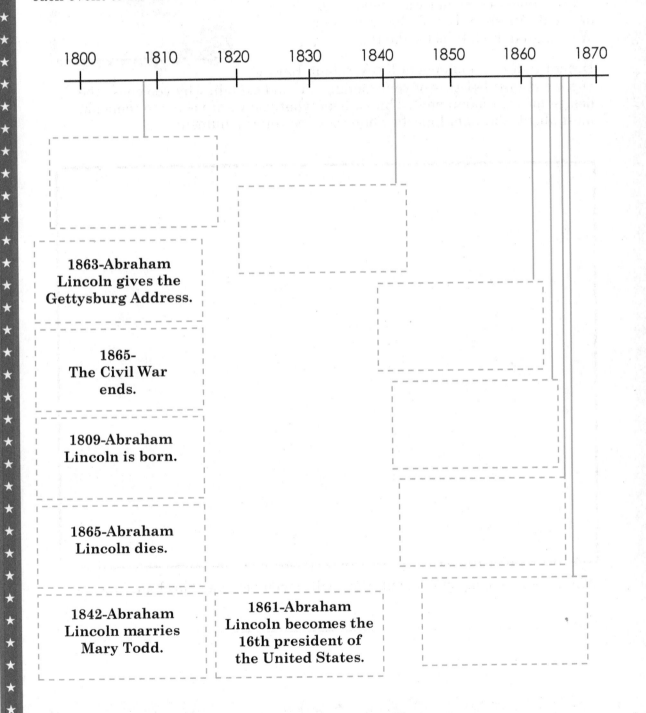

1800   1810   1820   1830   1840   1850   1860   1870

1863-Abraham Lincoln gives the Gettysburg Address.

1865-The Civil War ends.

1809-Abraham Lincoln is born.

1865-Abraham Lincoln dies.

1842-Abraham Lincoln marries Mary Todd.

1861-Abraham Lincoln becomes the 16th president of the United States.

⟳ Abraham Lincoln ⟳

Design a Monument

A monument is a sculpture or a building that helps people to remember an important person or event. Abraham Lincoln has a monument in Washington, D.C. It looks like this.

Design your own monument for Abraham Lincoln.
Draw a detailed picture of your monument, and explain why you chose the design for your monument. Think about what you want people to remember most about Abraham Lincoln when they see your monument.

When people see my monument, they will remember that Abraham Lincoln

was _____

_____ .

Painting a Portrait of President Lincoln

Use the color key to color this portrait of Abraham Lincoln.

KEY
1-gray 2-white 3-black 4-peach 5-red

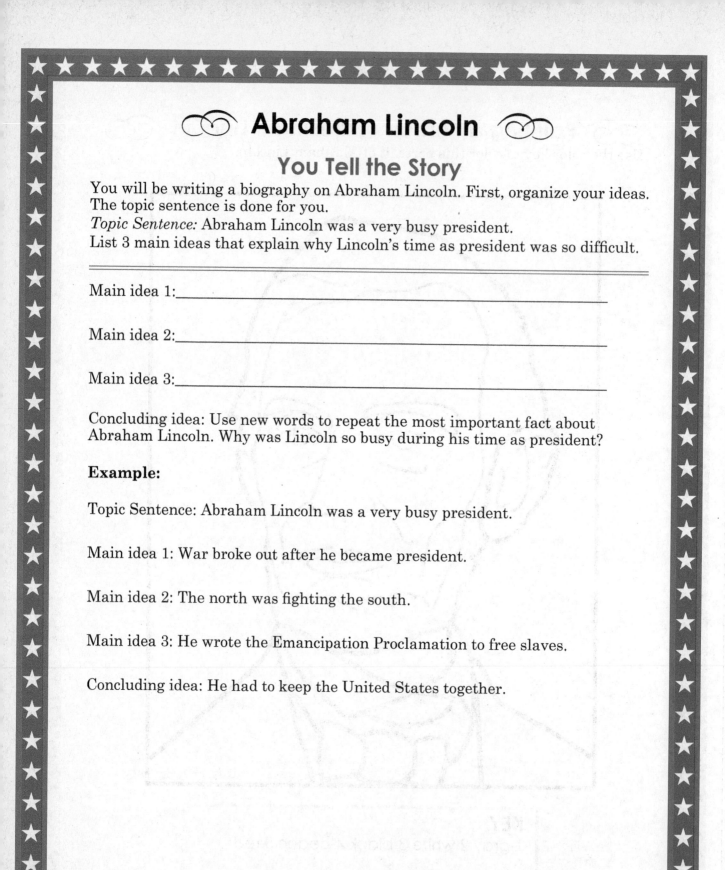

∞ Abraham Lincoln ∞

You Tell the Story

You will be writing a biography on Abraham Lincoln. First, organize your ideas. The topic sentence is done for you.

Topic Sentence: Abraham Lincoln was a very busy president.

List 3 main ideas that explain why Lincoln's time as president was so difficult.

_____

Main idea 1:_____

Main idea 2:_____

Main idea 3:_____

Concluding idea: Use new words to repeat the most important fact about Abraham Lincoln. Why was Lincoln so busy during his time as president?

Example:

Topic Sentence: Abraham Lincoln was a very busy president.

Main idea 1: War broke out after he became president.

Main idea 2: The north was fighting the south.

Main idea 3: He wrote the Emancipation Proclamation to free slaves.

Concluding idea: He had to keep the United States together.

⮂ Abraham Lincoln ⮀

You Tell the Story

Now it is time to put your ideas together.

Abraham Lincoln was_____
Topic Sentence

Main idea 1

First, he_____

_____

_____.

Main idea 2

He also_____

_____

_____.

Main idea 3

Last, he _____

_____

_____.

Concluding idea

As you can see, _____

_____

_____

ᴄ⭘ Barack Obama ⭘ᴄ

Finding the Facts

Barack Obama was elected to be the 44th president of the United States of America. Read about the challenges and success that Barack Obama has had in his life. After you read, complete the sentences.

Barack Obama is the son of an African man and an American woman. His father was born in a little village in the country of Kenya. His mother was from a small town in the state of Kansas. When they met, Barack's parents were both going to college in Hawaii. Barack Obama was born in Hawaii on August 4, 1961. When Barack was very young, his father moved back to Kenya, and his mother raised him on her own in Hawaii and Indonesia. When he was 10 years old, Barack moved in with his grandparents. He lived with them in Hawaii, and he spent his days studying, body surfing, and playing basketball. Barack went to college in Los Angeles and New York. As time went on, he earned a law degree from Harvard. Barack Obama met Michelle Robinson when he was living in Chicago. They married and had two daughters, Malia and Sasha. Obama was a

civil rights lawyer and a law professor. He served for eight years as a state senator for Illinois. Today, Barack Obama is our 44th president, and the first African-American president of the United States. He was reelected to the office in November 2012 and is currently serving his second term. When he can find the time, President Obama still loves a good game of basketball.

1) Barack Obama was born in _____.

2) Barack Obama was elected to be our _____ president.

3) Barack Obama is the first _____ president of the United States.

4) President Obama lives in the White House with his wife, _____,

and his daughters, _____ and _____.

5) President Obama's favorite sport to play is _____.

A Timeline for Barack Obama

Barack Obama's Life

Match the correct year and event with the space on the timeline. Draw a line from each event to its correct box on the timeline.

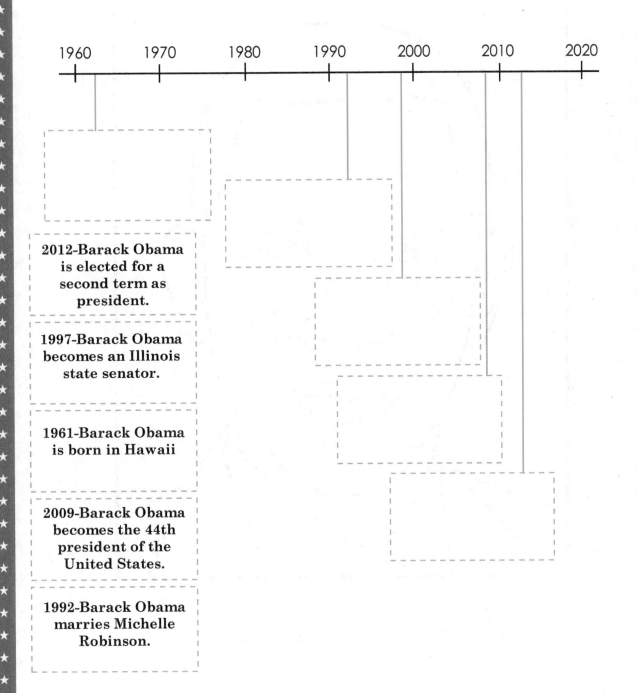

1960   1970   1980   1990   2000   2010   2020

2012-Barack Obama is elected for a second term as president.

1997-Barack Obama becomes an Illinois state senator.

1961-Barack Obama is born in Hawaii

2009-Barack Obama becomes the 44th president of the United States.

1992-Barack Obama marries Michelle Robinson.

Painting a Portrait of President Obama

Use the color key to color this portrait of Barack Obama.

KEY
1-brown 2-white 3-black 4-blue 5-red

Put on Your Thinking Cap for President Obama

Use the Venn Diagrams below to compare the life of President Obama to the lives of President George Washington and President Abraham Lincoln. Write each phrase in the correct sections of the Venn Diagrams.

Born in Hawaii
President of U.S.
Born in Virginia
Lawyer
Surveyor

Raised two children
Was married
Was president during the Civil War
Born in Kentucky

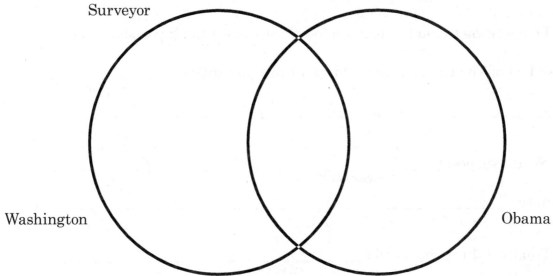

Washington   Obama

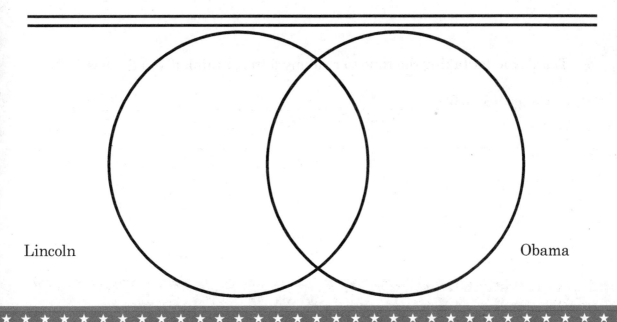

Lincoln   Obama

Barack Obama

Making Suggestions

Think about three things you think President Barack Obama should do as president of the United States. Write a letter to President Obama and tell him why you think these things are important. As a concluding sentence, explain how doing these three things will make Barack Obama a better president.

Dear Mr. President,

I am writing to you to suggest a few things that I think you should do as

president of The United States. First, I think you should _____
                                                            Suggestion #1
_____ because _____.

Next, I suggest you_____
                        Suggestion #2
because_____.

Finally, I think you should _____
                              Suggestion #3
_____.

Thank you for taking the time to read my letter. I think if you do these

three things, you will _____
                         Concluding Sentence
_____.

Sincerely, _____
                    Your name

Great job!

is an Education.com reading superstar

TRACING
YOUR ROOTS

How Are We Alike?

Pick a relative and find out about the things you share. Write the things only you like in the "Me" circle and the things only your relative likes in the other circle marked "Relative." Write down the things you both like in the space between.

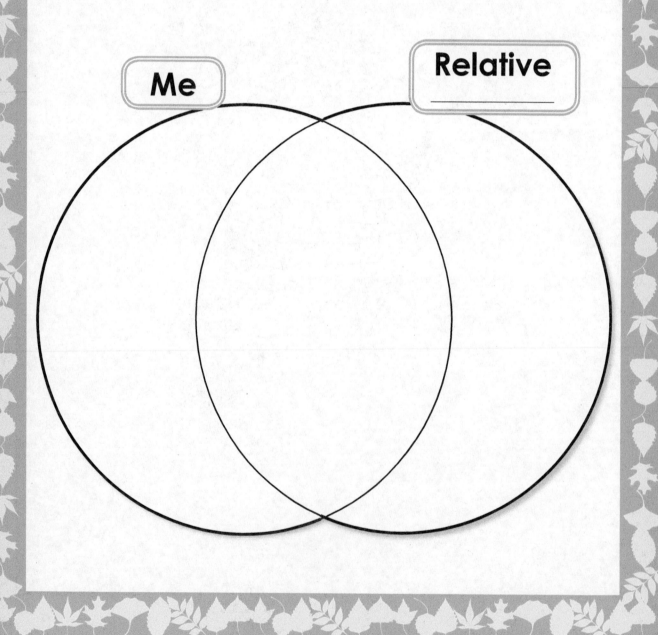

Descendant Chart

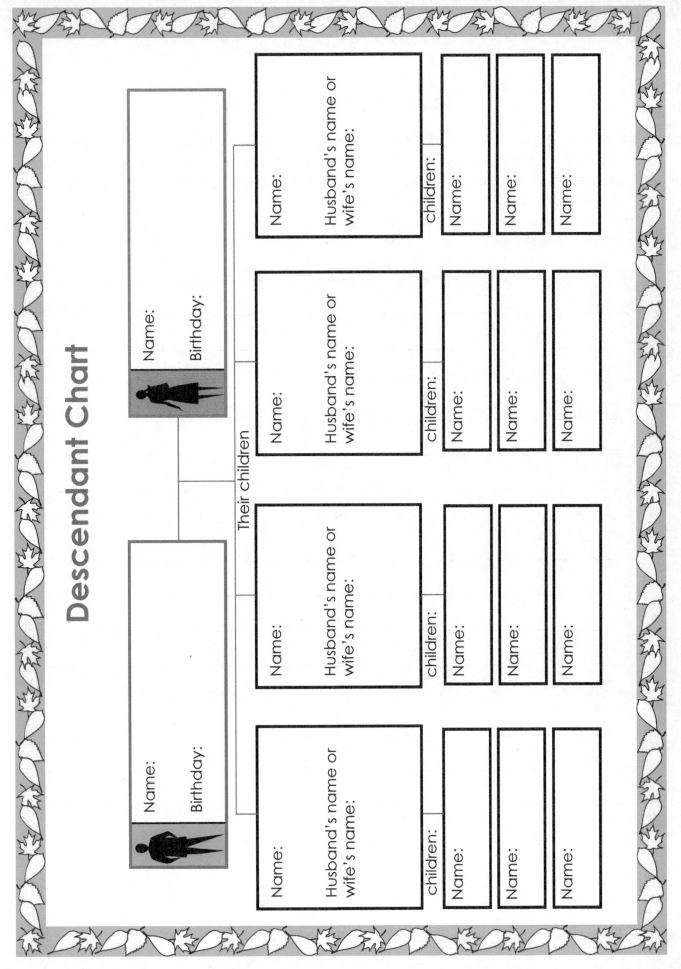

Name:

Birthday:

Name:

Birthday:

Their children

Name:

Husband's name or wife's name:

children:

Name:

Name:

Name:

Name:

Husband's name or wife's name:

children:

Name:

Name:

Name:

Name:

Husband's name or wife's name:

children:

Name:

Name:

Name:

Name:

Husband's name or wife's name:

children:

Name:

Name:

Name:

What's in a Name?

Parents often spend a lot of time choosing a name for their child. Sometimes they pick a name in honor of another family member or friend, sometimes the name they pick is popular or has a special meaning. Why did your parents choose your name? It's time to find out!

Ask your parents why they choose your first name. Write your notes below.

_____

_____

_____

Ask your parents why they choose your middle name. Write your notes below.

_____

_____

_____

Now find out why your parents have their names. Write your notes below.

_____

_____

_____

Find out why your grandparents have their names. Write your notes below.

_____

_____

_____

Family Interview: Personal History

Life was different when your parents were young and when your grandparents were young. Find out what their lives were like by asking these questions.

Name of person interviewed: _____

1. What was happening in the world when you were my age?

_____

_____

2. What is one of your strongest memories from that time?

_____

_____

3. What did you think you would be when you grew up?

_____

_____

4. What kinds of work did you end up doing?

_____

_____

_____

Add a drawing, photo, or artifact that helps to tell the story of your relative.

Mapping Your Family: North America

Your family may come from lots of different places. Color the places in North America where members of your family were born or where they lived. Remember to include your grandparents and your aunts and uncles!

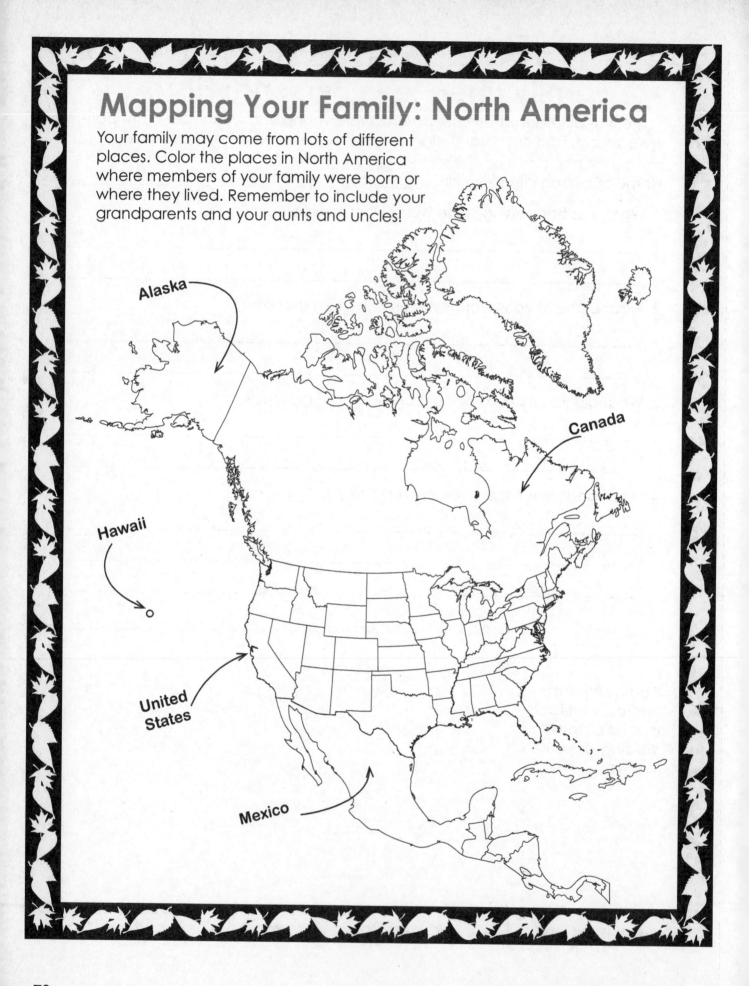

Alaska

Canada

Hawaii

United States

Mexico

Family Interview: Home Life

Life was different when your parents were young and when your grandparents were young. Find out what their lives were like by asking these questions.

Name of person interviewed: _____

1. What was it like where you grew up?

_____

_____

2. What was school like for you?

_____

_____

3. What chores did you have?

_____

_____

4. What were family meals like?

_____

_____

Add a drawing, photo, or artifact that helps to tell the story of your relative.

Recipes are a tasty way to follow a family's history. Use the cards below to write a recipe from someone in your family.

Our Family Recipe

Recipe name: _____

Ingredients

Directions

Who is this recipe from? _____

Why is this recipe special? _____

Our Family Recipe

Recipe name: _____

Ingredients

Directions

Who is this recipe from? _____

Why is this recipe special? _____

Family Interview: Family Fun

Life was different when your parents were young and when your grandparents were young. Find out what their lives were like by asking these questions.

Name of person interviewed: _____

1. What kind of music did you listen to?

   _____

   _____

2. What kind of clothes did you wear?

   _____

   _____

3. What were some of your favorite movies, TV programs or radio shows when you were my age?

   _____

   _____

4. What kinds of games and activities did your family like to do for fun?

   _____

   _____

   _____

Add a drawing, photo, or artifact that helps to tell the story of your relative.

Make a Time Capsule

We've all seen the movies where a group of kids digs up a mysterious box only to find treasures from the past inside. Wouldn't your second grader love to tell future generations of kids what it was like to live in your time? In the process, she will form a concrete understanding of what it means to set a purpose and consider the audience—two common language arts goals that can seem somewhat vague to students. Ask your second grader to reflect on the past year, gather her cool stuff and create a time capsule. Don't worry - she won't lose any of her valuable treasures in this activity. Instead, she'll gain some valuable writing tools!

What You Need:

- Shoe box
- Construction paper
- Glue stick
- Markers
- Magazines

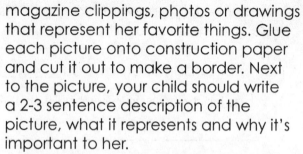

What You Do:

Explain the time capsule project to your child: one hundred years from now, second graders will want to know what it was like to be in this grade "back then." Your child can send a message to these kids of the future by creating a time capsule in which she describes all the things second graders love to do!

The next step is to gather the items for the time capsule. Your child should make a list of favorite activities, hobbies, sports, friends, school subjects, technology, etc. Then she should use magazine clippings, photos or drawings that represent her favorite things. Glue each picture onto construction paper and cut it out to make a border. Next to the picture, your child should write a 2-3 sentence description of the picture, what it represents and why it's important to her.

Remind your child that the purpose of her writing is to let future generations know what today's second graders like to do. Even if she writes about unique activities that are important to her (for example, playing the clarinet), encourage her to include activities and items that many second graders enjoy.

Remember, of course: life may be very different for students a hundred years hence, and they may have never seen any of the items in the time capsule. She should keep the audience in mind and write detailed descriptions of the items. Encourage your child to include newspaper clippings about current world, national and local events. Who was president of the United States this year? What were the hottest baseball and football teams? What's the latest technology for kids and for adults? What two problems do people around your community worry about the most? What are five popular foods, and how much does it cost to buy them at a restaurant?

The final step is to bury the time capsule! Help your child pick a spot in the yard or the garden and "plant" her time capsule. Explain that in one hundred years, your backyard might be a park and kids digging in the sandbox will be thrilled to discover a treasure from the past!

Make Your Family Crest

In the past, crests were used by nobility to represent a person or family. Now you can make your own crest for your family. Draw items in the crest below that have meaning to your family, such as animals, food or favorite things. At the bottom, you can also write a family motto. A motto is a phrase that tells about your family. When you have drawn your crest, color it and it's done!

Motto

My Family Tree

Fill in the box at the bottom with your name, then write the names of your parents, grandparents and great-grandparents. You can also add their birthdays and where they were born.

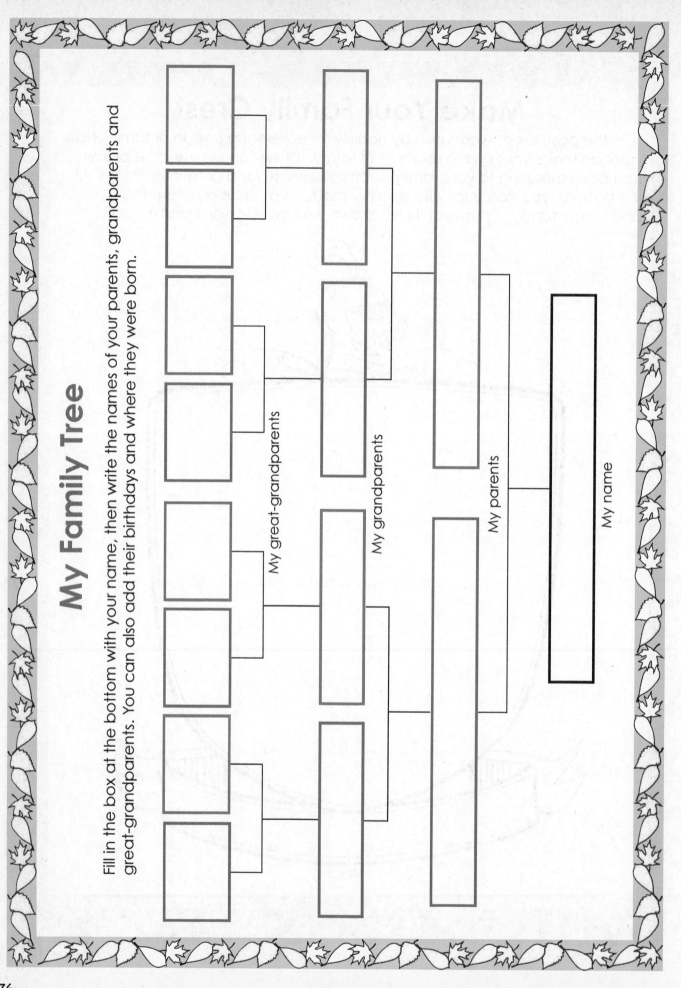

My great-grandparents

My grandparents

My parents

My name

The Movie of Us!

Ask your parents or grandparents to tell the story of how they met. Use the storyboard below to tell their story of how they fell in love in six frames, using words and/or pictures. You can start with the real story and then liven it up to make an epic love story suitable for the big screen!

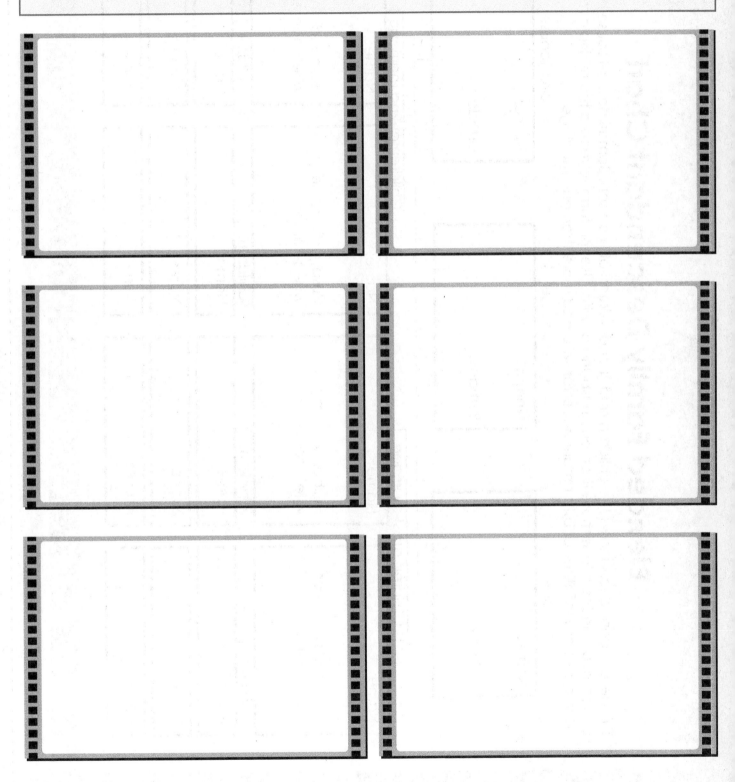

Blended Family Descendant Chart

This descendant chart shows the children and grandchildren of a person. Sometimes, because of a divorce or death, an ancestor has more than one husband or wife. Use this form to record the multiple marriages of your father, grandfather, or other male ancestor who had more than one marriage.

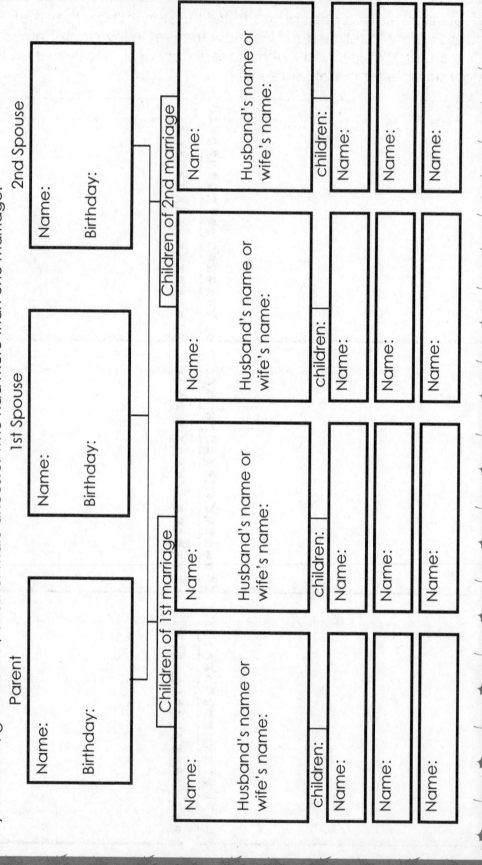

Parent

Name:

Birthday:

1st Spouse

Name:

Birthday:

2nd Spouse

Name:

Birthday:

Children of 1st marriage

Name:

Husband's name or wife's name:

children:

Name:

Name:

Name:

Name:

Husband's name or wife's name:

children:

Name:

Name:

Name:

Children of 2nd marriage

Name:

Husband's name or wife's name:

children:

Name:

Name:

Name:

Name:

Husband's name or wife's name:

children:

Name:

Name:

Name:

Family Word Search

Circle each word from the list in the puzzle.
The words can go any direction.

```
P  R  Y  Z  C  Z  W  B  P  N  I  D
U  I  Z  G  F  P  S  T  V  O  N  A
N  I  S  U  O  C  M  N  F  V  F  U
R  E  H  T  O  M  D  N  A  R  G  G
G  R  A  N  D  F  A  T  H  E  R  H
H  Y  C  U  R  E  H  T  O  R  B  T
U  L  H  N  O  S  F  T  N  U  A  E
S  I  I  L  B  A  E  C  E  I  N  R
B  M  L  P  T  R  E  H  T  O  M  J
A  A  D  H  W  E  H  P  E  N  S  K
N  F  E  R  E  T  S  I  S  J  Y  O
D  R  M  P  D  Q  U  N  C  L  E
```

AUNT	FATHER	NIECE
BROTHER	GRANDFATHER	SISTER
CHILD	GRANDMOTHER	SON
COUSIN	HUSBAND	UNCLE
DAUGHTER	MOTHER	
FAMILY	NEPHEW	

My Family's Heirloom

An heirloom is an object that has belonged to a family for a long time. An heirloom is often from an older family member, like a grandmother or aunt, who gives it to a younger family member. Jewelry, quilts and pictures are common heirlooms.

Draw or paste a picture of one of your family's heirlooms in the space below. Then answer the questions about the object.

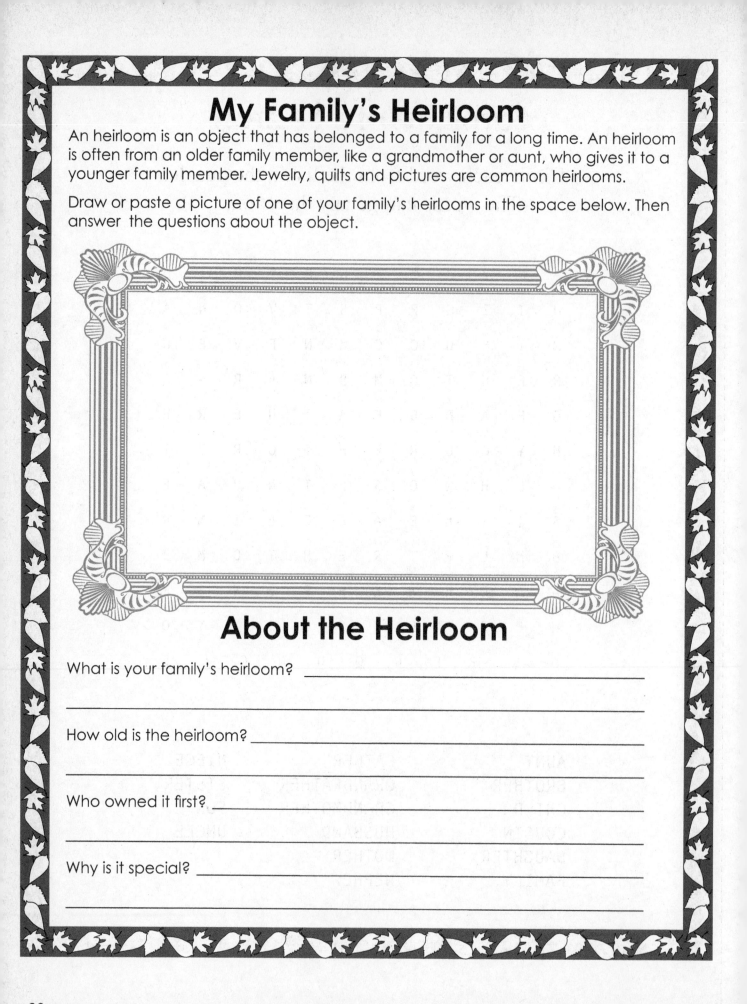

About the Heirloom

What is your family's heirloom? _____

_____

How old is the heirloom? _____

_____

Who owned it first? _____

_____

Why is it special? _____

_____

Honor an Ancestor!

In this activity you will try to get to know a long ago ancestor that you have never met! It is important to choose an ancestor that is somewhat known to your family — either through photographs, artifacts, or stories.

Name: _____

Dates: _____

Place of birth: _____

Career: _____

⬥ Ask your relatives for any other information that is known about your ancestor. Write your notes below.

_____

_____

_____

⬥ Look at a photo or other artifact from your ancestor. What information can you gather from it? Write your notes below.

_____

_____

_____

⬥ Research to find out any additional information about the place and time in which your ancestor lived. Write your notes below.

_____

_____

_____

Honor an Ancestor: Let's Plan a Party!

Let's plan a party in honor of one of your ancestors! Answer the questions below about what your ancestor would like. Then decorate the room below for a party. Be sure and draw in the decorations, food and games you think your ancestor would have liked.

Ancestor's name _____
_____

What kind of foods did your ancestor like to eat?_____
_____

What colors did your ancestor like?_____
_____

What kind of music would your ancestor like at the party? _____
_____

What games would your ancestor like to play at the party?_____
_____

Great job!

is an Education.com writing superstar

ANSWERS

She's So Cool - *Answers*

Julia Morgan   page 3

1.   Where did Julia Morgan build her buildings?
     Julia Morgan built her buildings in California.

2.   What did she like to study in school?
     In high school, she liked to study math.

3.   Why did the school in Paris turn her down?
     The school turned her down because she was a woman.

4.   Why did the Fairmont Hotel in San Francisco need to be rebuilt?
     The hotel was damaged in the 1906 earthquake.

5.   What is Julia's most famous building?
     Her most famous building is Hearst Castle.

Deborah Sampson   page 9

(**Early Life**)   (**Deborah in Disguise**)   (**The Fight's Not Over**)   (**A Lasting Legacy**)

1: When a good soldier is allowed to leave service, it is called an honorable discharge.
2: A payment that is given every month.

Sojourner Truth   page 10

1.   What year did Sojourner Truth escape?   **She escaped in 1826.**

2.   What happened to Sojourner Truth in 1850?   **In 1850, her biography was published.**

3.   Why do you think she wanted rights for women as well as an end to slavery?
     (many possible answers)

She's So Cool - *Answers*

Bessie Coleman and Mae Jemison   page 13

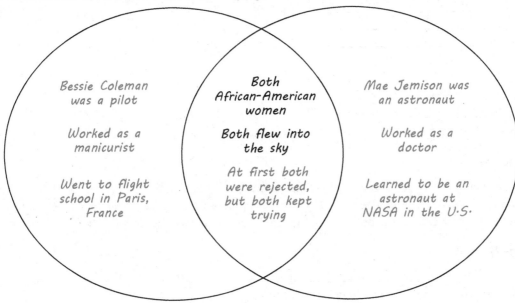

Bessie Coleman was a pilot

Worked as a manicurist

Went to flight school in Paris, France

Both African-American women

Both flew into the sky

At first both were rejected, but both kept trying

Mae Jemison was an astronaut

Worked as a doctor

Learned to be an astronaut at NASA in the U.S.

Juana Ines de la Cruz   page 14

Juana Ines de la Cruz was born on _____ **November 12, 1651** _in_ **San Miguel Nepantia, Mexico** .
Juana loved to _____ **learn** _____ and had to hide in a _____ **chapel** _____ so she could do so
without getting in trouble.

When she was older, she was sent to live in **Mexico City** . She wanted to
_____ **dress as a boy** _____ so that she could go to school, but her mother
wouldn't let her. Instead, her mother hired a _____ **tutor** _____ .
In _____ **1667** _____ , she became a nun so that she would be allowed to study. While she was a nun,
she wrote _____ **books** _____ , _____ **poems** _____ , and
_____ **plays** _____ that showed smart and brave women.

Ada Lovelace   page 15

Ada Lovelace was born in 1815 in London to Anne Isabella Byron and the famous poet, Lord
Byron. When she was a child, her mother encouraged her to study math, which was unusual for a
woman at the time. In 1833, she met mathematician Charles Babbage at a party. Charles had
been making a machine that could calculate math problems. Once he found out she was interested in math, they became good friends. He showed the machine to her and she was fascinated by
it. Charles then took Ada under his wing and taught her about his research during the next
several years.

About ten years later, Charles had an idea for a new mathematical machine. A fellow scientist had
written an article about it, but it was written in French. Charles asked Ada to translate the article
for him. Not only did she translate the article, she added her own notes and ideas. Many of her
ideas are still used in computers today. Her work went unnoticed until many years later, when
scientists realized how revolutionary her ideas were. Now, she is considered by many to be the
world's first computer programmer.

American Heroes – <u>Answers</u>

Abraham Lincoln **page 24**

1. Lincoln was born in the state of _____KENTUCKY_____ .
2. Lincoln once worked as a _____LAWYER_____ .
3. Lincoln's wife's name was _____MARY_____ .

John Adams **page 25**

1. Adams was also the first _____VICE_____ President.
2. Adams' son, John _____QUINCY_____ Adams, was the 6th President of the United States.
3. Adams was the only one of the first five Presidents who did not own ____SLAVES____ .

Alexander Hamilton **page 26**

1. Hamilton fought on the side of the American colonies in the _____REVOLUTIONARY_____ War.
2. He fought under General George ____WASHINGTON___ , who was so impressed that he gave Hamilton a job as his aide.
3. Hamilton wanted to create a strong _____FEDERAL____ , or national, government for the United States..

Eleanor Roosevelt **page 27**

1. Eleanor was also the wife of President _____FRANKLIN_____ D. Roosevelt.
2. Her humanitarian work changed the way America thought about what a _____FIRST_____ Lady could be.
3. Roosevelt spoke for the U.S. as a member of the ____UNITED____ Nations, a group of countries from around the world who work or peace and security for all nations.

Susan B. Anthony **page 28**

1. The right of women to vote in elections is called women's ___SUFFRAGE___ .
2. Anthony helped pass the 13th Amendment, which _____EMANCIPATED_____ or freed, all of the slaves.
3. In the last public speech of her life, Anthony inspired those working for women's rights by saying, "Failure is ___IMPOSSIBLE__ ."

Lorraine Hansberry **page 29**

1. <u>A Raisin in the Sun</u> was also the first play on Broadway with an African-American ___DIRECTOR___ , Lloyd Richards .
2. The 1961 film version of <u>A Raisin in the Sun</u> starred legendary African-American actor Sidney _____POITIER____ .
3. A 2004 Broadway revival of <u>A Raisin in the Sun</u> , starring Sean "_____DIDDY_____" Combs, received a Tony Award nomination for Best Revival of a Play.

Maya Angelou **page 30**

1. Angelou is a highly trained dancer who studied and performed with famed African-American choreographer Alvin ___AILEY___ .
2. One of her books of poetry, Just Give Me a Cool Drink of Water 'Fore I Diiiie, was nominated for a ___PULITZER__ Prize.
3. Angelou recited her poem, "On the Pulse of Morning," at the ___INAUGURATION___ ceremony for President Bill Clinton.

Celia Cruz **page 31**

1. Cruz recorded albums with some of the most famous musicians in _____LATIN_____ music.
2. "Salsa" is not only the name for a kind of music, but also for a kind of _____DANCE_____
3. Cuba is an island nation in a part of the ocean called the __CARIBBEAN__ Sea.

Rosa Parks **page 32**

1. Until the boycott, African-Americans in Alabama had to sit at the _____BACK_____ of the bus.
2. Rosa Parks became one of the most important leaders of the _____CIVIL_____ Rights Movement.
3. African-Americans were also banned from eating at some _____RESTAURANTS_____ , and from many other places..

American Heroes - <u>Answers</u>

Frederick Douglass **page 33**

1. Douglass sometimes gave President ___<u>LINCOLN</u>___ advice.
2. He wanted to give African-Americans the right to ____<u>VOTE</u>____.
3. Douglass was ambassador to the nation of ____<u>HAITI</u>____.

Booker T. Washington **page 34**

1. Booker T. Washington wrote a famous book about his life growing up, called "Up from ___<u>SLAVERY</u>___".
2. Though she herself could not read or write, Washington's ___<u>MOTHER</u>___, bought him textbooks so he could learn..
3. As a slave, Washington worked on a ___<u>PLANTATION</u>___, the type of farm on which most slaves were forced to work..

Jesse Owens **page 35**

1. The 1936 Summer Olympics took place in the German capital city of _____<u>BERLIN</u>_____.
2. Adi Dassler, the founder of athletic shoe company Adidas, persuaded Owens to wear Adidas shoes in the Olympic Games. This was the first known __<u>SPONSORSHIP</u>__ of an African-American athlete.
3. Owens' family moved from their home in Ohio during the Great __<u>MIGRATION</u>__ when many African-Americans moved away from the South.

W.E.B. DuBois **page 36**

1. Du Bois worked to disprove the theory that African-Americans were biologically inferior to white Americans, called __<u>SCIENTIFIC</u>__ racism.
2. Du Bois was one of the founders of the NAACP, the National Association for the ___<u>ADVANCEMENT</u>___ of Colored People.
3. In 1950, Du Bois ran for U.S. ___<u>SENATOR</u>___ from New York as a member of the American Labor Party.

Martin Luther King, Jr. **page 37**

1. His life as an activist began with the ____<u>MONTGOMERY</u>____ Bus Boycott, started by Rosa Parks in the city it is named for.
2. Martin Luther King, Jr. was ___<u>ASSASSINATED</u>___ on April 4, 1968 in Memphis, Tennessee..
3. In 1983, a __<u>FEDERAL</u>__ holiday was declared in honor of Martin Luther King, Jr. We still observe that holiday every January.

George Washington Carver **page 38**

1. Though he is often falsely credited with having invented ____<u>PEANUT BUTTER</u>____ Carver did create more than 300 products using peanuts.
2. Carver's birthplace was declared a national _____<u>MONUMENT</u>_____, the first ever dedicated to an African-American.
3. Many leaders consulted with Carver over agricultural matters, from Presidents of the United States to the Crown Prince of the country of____<u>SWEDEN</u>____.

Lewis and Clark **page 39**

1. Another goal of the expedition was to make friends and set up trade with ___<u>NATIVE</u>___ American tribes.
2. __<u>SACAGAWEA</u>__ a Native American woman who knew the territory, helped guide the expedition.
3. Along the way, Lewis and Clark saw many kinds of plants and __<u>ANIMALS</u>___ they had never seen before..

Benjamin Franklin **page 40**

1. Using a metal key tied to a kite, Franklin proved that lightning conducts _____<u>ELECTRICITY</u>_____.
2. Franklin is responsible for the famous saying, "A penny saved is a penny ____<u>EARNED</u>____."
3. Franklin believed all people should be free, and spoke out against the practice of ____<u>SLAVERY</u>____.

Thomas Edison **page 41**

1. Edison created one of the first electric __<u>UTILITIES</u>__ companies.
2. He had over 1,000 ___<u>PATENTS</u>___, which give rights and credit for inventions to their creator.
3. Edison also invented new ways of filming a _____<u>MOTION PICTURE</u>_____ also known as a movie.

George Washington

Finding the Facts

George Washington is known as the "Father of Our Country". Read about George Washington to see why he was given this nickname. After you read, complete the sentences.

George Washington was born in Virginia on February 22, 1732. At this time, America was ruled by England. When he was a young boy, George had to travel a very long distance to get to school. To get to his first school, George had to walk seven miles each way. George studied hard and became a surveyor. A surveyor is someone who measures land and makes maps. George Washington's home was a farm called Mount Vernon. As an adult, he married a woman named Martha Custis. Martha had two children, and George helped raise them. At this time, there were a lot of people living in America who did not want America to be part of England anymore. George Washington was chosen to be the Commander in Chief of the American army. He fought in the Revolutionary War so that America could be a separate country. After a long and difficult fight, America won the war and gained its independence from England. It became the United States of America, and George Washington was elected as the first president in 1789. At that time, the capital of the United States was New York. The capital later became Washington, D.C., named for George Washington.

1) When George Washington was born, America was ruled by _____England_____.

2) George Washington's first job was as a surveyor. A surveyor is someone who

_____Someone who measures land and makes maps_____

3) George Washington's home was called _____Mount Vernon_____.

4) Martha Custis was the _____wife_____ of George Washington.

5) George Washington was the Commander in Chief of

the_____American_____ army.

page 46

A Timeline for George Washington

George Washington's Life

Cut and paste the events, and place them in the correct order on the timeline. Match the correct year and event with the space on the timeline.

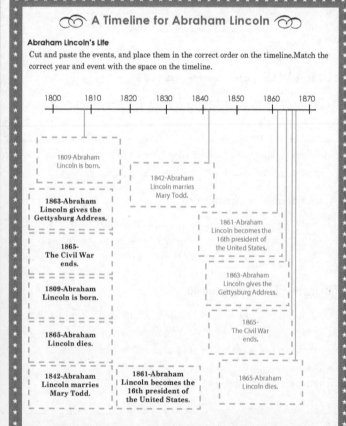

1730 1740 1750 1760 1770 1780 1790 1800

1732- GeorgeWashington is born.

1759- George marries Martha Custis.

1776-America declares independence from England.

1789- George Washington is elected the first president of the U.S.

1799- George Washington dies.

1732- GeorgeWashington is born.

1776-America declares independence from England.

1799- George Washington dies.

1759- George marries Martha Custis.

1789- George Washington is elected the first president of the U.S.

page 47

Abraham Lincoln

Finding the Facts

Abraham Lincoln was our 16th president and often called "Honest Abe." Read about Abraham Lincoln to learn why he is one of our most well-known presidents. After you read, complete the sentences.

Abraham Lincoln was born in a log cabin the state of Kentucky on February 12, 1809. He and his sister worked on their family farm. When his family moved to Indiana, Abe helped build the family's new home. Abe didn't get to go to school very often, but he loved to read, and he would walk miles to borrow books. When he grew up, Abe had many different jobs. He was a shopkeeper and a mailman. Finally, Abe decided to study law, became a lawyer, and moved to Springfield, Illinois. There, he married Mary Todd. Abe and Mary had four children. In 1860, Abraham Lincoln was elected to be our 16th president. While he was president, the Civil War began. Our country was divided. The northern states were fighting against the southern states. During the war, Abraham Lincoln wrote the Emancipation Proclamation, which freed slaves. He also wrote a very famous speech called the Gettysburg Address. President Lincoln gave this speech to try to keep the United States together. The war lasted five years, and President Lincoln was killed just five days after the war ended. The United States had lost their president. and President Lincoln was killed just five days after the war ended. The United States had lost their president.

1) Abraham Lincoln was born in a _____log cabin_____.

2) More than anything, Abraham Lincoln loved to _____read_____.

3) Abraham Lincoln studied law and became a _____lawyer_____.

4) Abraham Lincoln was elected to be our _____16th_____ president in 1860.

5) Lincoln was president during the _____Civil_____ War.

page 52

A Timeline for Abraham Lincoln

Abraham Lincoln's Life

Cut and paste the events, and place them in the correct order on the timeline. Match the correct year and event with the space on the timeline.

1800 1810 1820 1830 1840 1850 1860 1870

1809-Abraham Lincoln is born.

1842-Abraham Lincoln marries Mary Todd.

1863-Abraham Lincoln gives the Gettysburg Address.

1861-Abraham Lincoln becomes the 16th president of the United States.

1865- The Civil War ends.

1863-Abraham Lincoln gives the Gettysburg Address.

1809-Abraham Lincoln is born.

1865- The Civil War ends.

1865-Abraham Lincoln dies.

1842-Abraham Lincoln marries Mary Todd.

1861-Abraham Lincoln becomes the 16th president of the United States.

1865-Abraham Lincoln dies.

page 53

∽ Barack Obama ∾

Finding the Facts

Barack Obama was elected to be the 44th president of the United States of America. Read about the challenges and success that Barack Obama has had in his life. After you read, complete the sentences.

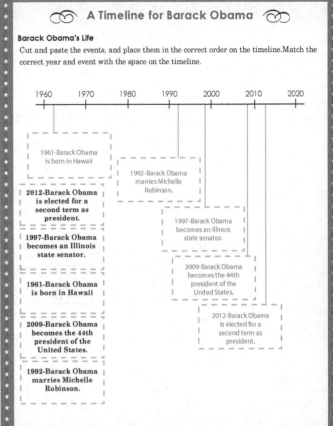

Barack Obama is the son of an African man and an American woman. His father was born in a little village in the country of Kenya. His mother was from a small town in the state of Kansas. When they met, Barack's parents were both going to college in Hawaii. Barack Obama was born in Hawaii on August 4, 1961. When Barack was very young, his father moved back to Kenya, and his mother raised him on her own in Hawaii and Indonesia. When he was 10 years old, Barack moved in with his grandparents. He lived with them in Hawaii, and he spent his days studying, body surfing, and playing basketball. Barack went to college in Los Angeles and New York. As time went on, he earned a law degree from Harvard. Barack Obama met Michelle Robinson when he was living in Chicago. They married and had two daughters, Malia and Sasha. Obama was a civil rights lawyer and a law professor. He served for eight years as a state senator for Illinois. Today, Barack Obama is our 44th president, and the first African-American president of the United States. He was reelected to the office in November 2012 and is currently serving his second term. When he can find the time, President Obama still loves a good game of basketball.

1) Barack Obama was born in _____Hawaii_____.

2) Barack Obama was elected to be our _____44th_____ president.

3) Barack Obama is the first _African American_ president of the United States.

4) President Obama lives in the White House with his wife, ___Michelle___,

and his daughters, _____Malia_____ and ____Sasha____.

5) President Obama's favorite sport to play is _basketball_____.

∽ A Timeline for Barack Obama ∾

Barack Obama's Life

Cut and paste the events, and place them in the correct order on the timeline. Match the correct year and event with the space on the timeline.

1960   1970   1980   1990   2000   2010   2020

1961-Barack Obama is born in Hawaii

1992-Barack Obama marries Michelle Robinson.

1997-Barack Obama becomes an Illinois state senator.

2009-Barack Obama becomes the 44th president of the United States.

2012-Barack Obama is elected for a second term as president.

2012-Barack Obama is elected for a second term as president.

1997-Barack Obama becomes an Illinois state senator.

1961-Barack Obama is born in Hawaii

2009-Barack Obama becomes the 44th president of the United States.

1992-Barack Obama marries Michelle Robinson.

∽ Put on Your Thinking Cap for President Obama ∾

Use the Venn Diagrams below to compare the life of President Obama to the lives of President George Washington and President Abraham Lincoln. Write each phrase in the correct sections of the Venn Diagrams.

Born in Hawaii
President of U.S.
Born in Virginia
Lawyer
Surveyor

Raised two children
Was married
Was president during the Civil War
Born in Kentucky

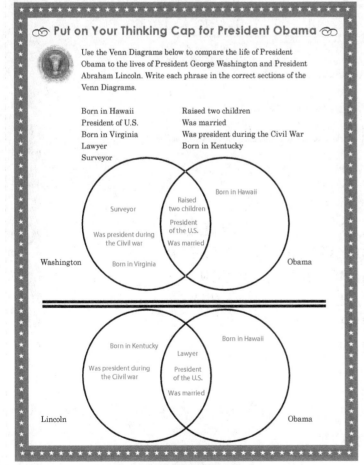

Washington
Surveyor
Was president during the Civil war
Born in Virginia
Raised two children
President of the U.S.
Was married
Born in Hawaii
Obama

Lincoln
Born in Kentucky
Was president during the Civil war
Lawyer
President of the U.S.
Was married
Born in Hawaii
Obama

Family Word Search

Circle each word from the list in the puzzle.
The words can go any direction.

```
P R Y Z C Z W B P N I D
U I Z G F P S T V O N A
N I S U O C M N F V F U
R E H T O M D N A R G G
G R A N D F A T H E R H
H Y C U R E H T O R B T
U L H N O S F T N U A E
S I I L B A E C E I N R
B M L P T R E H T O M J
A A D H W E H P E N S K
N F E R E T S I S J Y O
D R M P D Q U N C L E
```

AUNT	FATHER	NIECE
BROTHER	GRANDFATHER	SISTER
CHILD	GRANDMOTHER	SON
COUSIN	HUSBAND	UNCLE
DAUGHTER	MOTHER	
FAMILY	NEPHEW	

page 79